I0482045

Simple
Social
Business

Written by Patrick Long
Owner of MODIFY MEDIA

This book will enable you to

Learn and understand the simplistic means of social media

Improve your customer care communications and build relationships online

Increase reachability within your online marketing strategies

Understand social media marketing

Learn affective content marketing techniques to create a self driven 'likeable' business

Discover how you can become a leading authority within your marketplace

Table of contents

- Snapchat

- Content marketing

- Addicted

- Email is not dead

- Mobile is winning

- Network = Net-worth

- Reference

Introduction

To start off, we are doing it all wrong. Life is simple, we choose to complicate things...
For example; 'social' media or 'social' networking sites are meant to be social, yet we choose to become addicts to scrolling, checking, liking and contributing to our own social profiles without actually socialising.

At no other point in human history have we been so connected, yet so unconnected.
Did you know? A study once suggested that people check their phones roughly 40 times per day, yet others say that the real number is closer to triple that amount. Did you also know? On average 61% of people who own a mobile phone check their phone within five minutes of waking up, roughly 80% within 30 minutes and over 90% within the hour of waking up.
All of these statistics are associated with social media usage, yes thats right the main reason the majority of people are checking their phones so fast is their addiction to social media.

Many believe that social media is one of the greatest internet advancement of our time, but on the other side there are those who feel social media has destroyed a generation and created mindless zombie like individuals craving attention like never seen before. Whilst both of these arguments stands to have a valid point, no one can deny that social media has huge financial benefits that have literally turned business upside down.

The old ways of marketing and advertising are appearing to slowly die out, with a product going viral and selling out overnight on social media. A product or service selling out overnight is a drastic example, but the idea of this ignites excitement within any business owner. Having your product or service be sought after so extensively must be a dream, as long as you can keep up with such high demand without damaging your brands availability or quality.

Although the idea of viral content and high spikes in profit is one of the main reasons businesses use social media, it has become more of a expense then it has a revenue stream. Majority of business owners are paying for advertising on each social media platform to try and achieve a good return on their advertising investment.
A big question should be, Is the cost of advertising on social media really a investment? as the definition of investment is: 'the action or process of investing money for profit.'

How many business owners are accumulating actual profits whilst paying for advertising on social media?
More worrying is the fact many businesses are paying for advertising on social media, to gain their business more attention and not more sales. This fundamentally is creating business owners, who are failing.

Lets face facts, we all want loads of attention, or to hit that viral content that will boost our sales to unimaginable heights. Yet many businesses seem to be paying for half assed ads and boosting posts, all for attention. We are yet to get past a few thousand likes that does not even equal sales figures.
Attention has become a bigger need then actual business responsibilities, like hitting targets and creating sales.

ENGAGMENT TIP:

—— MODIFY MEDIA TOP TIPS ——

Polls: Facebook offers built-in polls, although running polls manually works best for boosting engagement
(e.g. "Which of these films is your favorite?")

Who are Modify Media?

Modify Media as a business was created for the simplicity of utilising images and videos online. Originally the business was to provide photography and videography services for all local businesses, yet a large gap come within the market that modify media could really flourish.

Meeting new clients who wanted new pictures and videos was fairly easy, but the majority of these clients had no idea how to use this content online. Each image you post represents your business, so posting blurry images and suggesting people buy your product or service is a terrible way to represent your business online.

After various training sessions and class room type settings, we decided it was our duty to supply learning material for all to use to maximise their reach and engagement online.
Remember it is not how much you post, but rather the quality of your posts that will help improve engagement and build relationships to which will increase sales.

Modify Media are approached regularly by a wide variety of businesses, charities and organisations, all of which are looking for social media marketing help and advice.
We have found a large majority of businesses are spending a unjust amount of time and money gaining 'likes', or 'followers' for no real reason. The first thing we must clarify is the return of profit or

value you are getting from each new 'like' or 'follower'.

One of the main aims for many business owners is to turn over a profit and become more financially secure.
Social media is by far one of the most valuable free sources of adverting a business can have, yet many use it to attract attention and hoping this added attention will some day lead to a customer.

Remember your customers, or potential customers should be bringing you profits or value. The concept of value is simple, value simply means a new sign up, or engagement of which brings value from a follower or potential customers.
Engagement is of great importance as a valuable customer is another source of added advertisement, every time they share, comment, or interact they further share your business, brand or product.

A valuable customer may be someone who has never made a purchase, but they may love your brand and share your content. This added team member is essentially bringing you potential profits without them actually purchasing any product or service.
Sharing your content and using word of mouth to bring potential customers your way, thats great value in one of your followers.
Your valuable potential customers will help you accumulate profits, all through the content you provide and they engage with.

Who is this book aimed at ?

Thats a good direct question and has a very simple answer.
This book is for everyone.
The reason the book is aimed at everyone, is the simple fact that social media growth is to big to ignore and at some point it will be larger then our imaginations can conceive right now.

As you read this book, Facebook is already funding projects to look into virtual reality social media connections and artificial intelligence. This may sound like something from a sci-fi movie but there is no bounds when it comes to technological advancements, especially when it comes to communication and social networking.

With these advancements in mind, this book is also mainly written for the purpose of advancing your social media knowledge to utilise within your business. Every tom, dick and harry is using social media for various reasons concerning business. The simple fact is, tom, dick and harry may not have the knowledge you do to excel online.

You must learn a whole array of marketing techniques and strategies to keep your head above the crowed. Although with that in mind, you may just want to blend in and just have a little more success then the competition within your town.

Either way, keeping up to date with the large amount of social media platforms is a full time job. We have compacted as much as we can into this book, for you to use as a reference.
You need to think outside of the box, to utilise whats inside the screen..
Take some time out and get stuck in..
If self education is the key to success, then this book is the key to success with your social media.

What is social media?

If you are not actively using social media personally updating the world about your life, then trying to use social media for your business is going to be a very new experience. Not only can new ways of advertising and marketing your business be very time costly, but this can also lead to being very expensive.
We shall take this from a amateur point of view, whilst giving a brief crash course in social media.

As we all know everyone is talking about social media, as if it was the hottest topic since the beginning of the internet. Well to be perfectly honest it is.
Social media has taken the world by storm, to which it is nearly impossible to have a business and not link that business to a social media platform of some sort.
Bill gates once said "If your business is not on the internet, then your business will be out of business". These are very wise words from once the richest man in the world.

We have now come to a age where "If your business is not on social media, is your business even a business?'.
We also live in a generation of which, if your personal relationship is not visible on social media many may question if that relationship is even 'official'... Its sad to say and even offensive.

So many are using social media to connect with businesses now days, its become something like the go to app to contact a business. If your looking for a certain event, business, venue, restaurant, then the first two places people look are Google and social media.

Here is something you should always remember when creating content, or using platforms online:
K.I.S.S = Keep It Simple Stupid.
Keeping your business simple to find and interact with, will improve your online engagement and increase sales.
It is common knowledge and phycological facts that consumers react positively to simplicity.

Take Facebook for example, there are so many external sites that let you sign up with your Facebook log in details.
Logging in to your Facebook account rather then joining external sites through the traditional registration processes.
No need for email address, phone number, passwords, etc, Simply sign into Facebook and you have signed up to a external website or app.
Facebook have made a process simple, of which allows them to gather even more information from its users.

Social media's definition is 'websites and applications that enable users to create and share content or to participate in social networking'.
Unfortunately for many people, social media is neither a place for content creation or social networking.

Social media for many is a time costly event, where we share some irrelevant or poor content irregularly and let our egos grow with the interactions to our content.
For others it is scrolling for hours, looking at other peoples content and feeling down about what they are producing or how they live.

We need to start seeing social media for what it really is and thats a direct line to people, businesses, networking opportunities and a place where we can all grow a audience whilst expressing ourselves and our businesses.
Social media can be the greatest place for you to grow, or it can be a time draining, depressing, or even a antisocial addiction.

CONTENT TIP:

———— MODIFY MEDIA TOP TIPS ————

Republish aka redistribute old content. There's no reason not to re share really good content you've done in the past, especially if you have valuable content.

The main stream media & social media..

Another popular definition of social media is by looking at normal main stream media. Main stream media is usually referred to as TV, newspapers, magazines and radio. All of these media outlets are a way of broadcasting to the masses.

Social media is exactly that, but with the social part in front, you get to interact with the content being distributed to the masses.
You get to act like the main stream media by broadcasting to the masses yourself online.

Thats what makes social media so addictive and exciting, not only do we get mass news and gossip but we can interact and connect with that content. Think of everything within the mainstream media, all the stories, heartache, celebrities, business and products we all want to hear more about, or become closer to these stories.
Well social media gives us a platform where we can get closer to all this, without costing us anything but time.

Although social media and mainstream media are separate, you can see the similarities an effectiveness of each. Main stream media has transitioned over to utilise social media, whilst social media has given individuals the power to do the same as the main stream media.

Main stream media is effectively the original form of broadcasting to the masses, todays social media can be your own platform for broadcasting to the masses...

In the beginning...

Originally main stream media was once TV, Radio and Newspapers. These broadcasting resources once used to reach the masses, with very little way of the masses reaching back.

The start of a evolution...

Main stream media then gained a larger audience when it was able to broadcast to the masses through the internet. Another resource of which it was able to broadcast.

Now we live in a connected world...

The main stream media is still able to broadcast to the masses through the internet today, via social media platforms. The big difference now is the masses can now broadcast back, whilst connecting with each other. Social media has now given anyone the ability to potentially broadcast to the masses.

TWITTER TIP:

—— MODIFY MEDIA TOP TIPS ——

Schedule tweets for evenings and weekends so you don't miss out on traffic.

The beginning of social media madness

Lets take a trip back in time to some social media back stories, to better understand what social media is. During the 70's Email was being developed, from a primitive form of electronic mail to a more sophisticated form of Email.
Around 1994 blogging was supposedly invented, but did not have the name 'blogging', it was referred to as a personal homepage.
In 1997 the real advancements came when blogging started taking off, to which many called it 'weblog'.
The first kinds of social media didn't materialise until around 1997, with individuals being able to create a profile and connect with other users profiles online.

It was in the 20th century that the internet really made advancements, that have changed the way we live. The world wide craze of social media was blossoming.

Lets leap forward to 2004 when Facebook was founded, to which many today class as one of the best ways to portray your business on social media. The argument can be had that Instagram is growing in popularity to become one of the best social media sites for business, but a know fact is Facebook own Instagram. Many features that are on Instagram are also available on Facebook, so many of your advertising campaigns can be linked.

Instagram was lunched in 2010 and was a fast growing successful social media app. Only two years later Instagram was then bought by Facebook in 2012 for $1 billion. Going from $0 to $1 billion is a very impressive move over a two year period, but whats more impressive is the fact that Mark Zuckerburg the Facebook founder is now roughly worth over $70 billion.

If you, or your business have a face for TV, then maybe YouTube is your thing, but if you are unfamiliar with YouTube then here is a back story. YouTube is the video sharing social media platform.
YouTube was founded in 2005, around the same time social media really started kicking off. Youtube was then bought just a year later by google for a cool $1.65 billion.

It is very clear that there is big money in social media, but what does YouTube offer its users? YouTube has over a billion users, with over 300 hours of video uploaded every minute.
YouTube is the second most used search engine online right behind Google.

YouTube is great for your business, because video's are becoming very popular online.
Bare in mind if your YouTube account was to become very popular, then you could potentially earn a revenue through the ads on your YouTube channel.

Lets take a leap over to Twitter now and see what all the tweeting is about. Tweeting is basically

what you do on twitter, its little messages you send and receive on your twitter profile.
Unfortunately and fortunately twitter only allows 280 characters to be placed into each tweet, which helps twitter stand out as a social media platform.
Whilst blogging on websites is all well and good for many, there is still a large amount who have no clue how to blog. This is when Twitter was once known as the 'microblogger', for the simplicity of sharing to the masses with ease.

Twitter was founded in 2006, which again is not far off the big boom of social media. Its clear that the beginning of the 20th century really was a wonderful and new world to be apart of.

There are plenty of other social media platforms you can choose from, but always remember where your target market will be. Not everyone uses every social media platform, so make sure you are using the right ones, to suit your goals.

CONTENT TIP:

——— MODIFY MEDIA TOP TIPS ———

Include imagery in your content where possible. People are much more likely to share this kind of content.

A general idea of some social media platforms would be:

News/Bookmarking:
Folkd
Reddit
Gather
Digg
Delicious

Music/video:
Soundcloud
YouTube
Snapchat

Images/video:
Flickr
Instagram
Pintrest
Snapchat

Popular:
Facebook
Instagram
Twitter
Snapchat

What is social media marketing?

Lets start of with the definition of social media marketing, which is: 'Social media marketing (SMM) refers to techniques that target social networks and applications to spread brand awareness or promote particular products. Social media marketing campaigns usually centre around: Establishing a social media presence on major platforms'.

Social media marketing sounds very simple when it is explained like that, well sort of simple..
The real question is how can you adapt social media marketing to your business?
Do you even have a social media marketing strategy in place?

You may be thinking that a butcher and a gym owner, may have different target audiences so how do the different social media marketing strategies work.
How do you choose the right strategy to expand your business through social media.
Lets take a step back and break down the two parts:

Social media = Websites and applications that enable users to create and share <u>content</u> or to participate in <u>social networking</u>.

Marketing = The action or business of promoting and selling products or services, including market research and advertising.

As you have a definition in the first half of this chapter, there is no need to combine the two aspects of social media marketing.
(We have underlined some key aspects in the above descriptions)

We have found that through various encounters with small and even larger companies, many still lack the knowledge to tackle a good marketing strategy online.
Looking at your business and now understanding what social media marketing is, you must challenge yourself to create a successful piece of content you can market.

As stated social media is about networking with your potential customers, whilst building your brand online.
A vast number of businesses fail at social media marketing because they lack the knowledge needed to create attractive, usable, likeable content.
Remember you are trying to market your product or services online, but you must build relationships and strengthen your brand at the same time.
Social media marketing is not just hard selling.

The bottom line is you want more customers, or clients to increase profit for your business.
Unfortunately for many of you, you portray your online profiles as hard selling platforms boasting about your product or service.

The big issue here is you lack the social networking aspect of social media, which then leads to losing customers rather then gaining.

Whilst loosing customers and scaring off potential customers, you are affectively doing your market research which in this case would produce false results.
Your market research at this stage would show that a handful of friends and family like your online business profiles, but few interact or share your content.
Also whilst conducting your market research for your product or service, you will find that there is very little desire for your product or service.

You have a social media platform of which is your social media side covered, you've started promoting and selling products which is the marketing side covered.
Why would you have a negative affect, or a neutral effect and not attract more customers? Simple. You are hard selling, when no one wants to be sold to.

Make your product or service so exciting, or interesting that you attract engagement then you can build from there. Build a audience and sell to them once you have captured their trust or interest.

Below is a example of how many businesses start out on social media:

 This represents your business, of which you decided to take online..

 Like many businesses you have a website already, your website has all your usual details of how to contact and find your business.

 You set up some social media accounts and start 'Social media marketing'.

 You are not getting the sales or feedback you desire from your social media efforts, so you decide paying for advertising on social media is a better way to market and sell.

 Whilst the advertising seems to be brining in a few extra irregular customers, or irregular sales your profit margins are lower due to fluctuations of your new advertising costs.

 From your experience and loss of money, you decide social media marketing is not what its made out to be. You decide to give social media a break for a while as its costing money, with little regular returns..

A big problem of social media marketing is, so many people believe that a good strategy is to simply post your offers and services online. Some businesses make the mistake of just paying for their social media business profile/page to be 'boosted'. This is another way to increase a reach slightly, but your real aim is your conversions to attract the right people who really will interact, buy and share your product or service

Yes we all want to earn more from our clients, or customers, but no one has come online to be sold to initially.
First rule of social media is you need to spark a interest and grab your potential customers attention, this will then give you a chance to build trust and relationships.

Building trust and relationships online will rapidly increase your growth and accountability, you will have much more success on social media if you are genuine and generic.

Your marketing campaigns should contain calls to action buttons, with a call to action you save yourself from being that ego obsessed business fishing for likes and followers.

TWITTER TIP:

——— MODIFY MEDIA TOP TIPS ———
Tweet daily. If you're not consistently posting content your followers will lose interest.

29

Below is a list of social media marketing fundamentals we would suggest you have for your business:

1. **Quality and value** content will gain a larger following then many of the sales posts you pay to boost on social media.
Your potential customers are on social media to connect with people, businesses, celebrities, gossip and browse. You are going to want to grab their attention with some value, this can be done by bringing them quality content.
Quality wins over quantity, so make sure you spark a interest from your new engaging followers. Regular interactions to your content will boost your engagement and reachability.

2. **Industry leader and compounding** is a vital part to building your brand online. The fact that you have chosen social media to maximise your reach and increase your profit, shows you are ready to express your business.
If you are aware of the compound affect you will know progress and success all take consistent control. By consistently releasing content online you begin the process of affective social media marketing.
Your content needs to portray you in a light of which you become a authority within your industry. Stay up to date with changes in your field and become the go to source for that industry.
This also falls into content marketing, by bringing value to your audience.

3. **Listening and building relationships** with those in your industry. Some of the principles within networking marketing is still highly relevant for you and your business online. Listening to your customers, is a very simplistic way to do market research. Connecting with your customers online, not only gains a trust but also installs a personal level to your business. People will feel at ease and more confident with your brand, if they have been listened or spoken to.

NETWORKING TIP:

—— MODIFY MEDIA TOP TIPS ——
Share other people's content. Make sure you keep shared content relevant and interesting,.

31

Why social media marketing matters

With roughly 2.34 billion people using social media, you can be sure that social media is the no.1 choice to reach the masses. Now with this vast amount of people on social media imagine the possibilities if you knew great social media marketing sales techniques. You would surly be a millionaire in no time selling to that many people. Social media marketing in its self can be beautiful and profitable, although done poorly this can destroy your business and weaken your brand.

Social media has really boomed since the early 20th century, of which has now become a phenomenon. Everyone and their cousin is using social media in one way or another.

Social media has now taken over the lives of the younger generation and created exponential opportunities within the business world.
Our business alone is one such business that has been created all around social media , we just happen to offer the visual side of production also. There is a enormous amount of businesses revolving around social media. You have content creation companies, social media marketing companies, or social media influencing companies, the list can go on and on.

The hurdle you do have is becoming successful online, whilst cutting the advertising costs within your business.
Sounds like a catch 22, as surly more advertising

means more business right?
Well.. No not always.

You can be paying for a enormous amount for advertising anywhere, but if your advert or marketing strategy sucks then you will receive little to no profit from your advertising campaign.

The same principles in advertising anywhere else, are the same on social media.
The big difference is on social media you are a click away from losing that potential customer, so you best stand out and grab some attention or you will lose a lot of customers fast.

You can literally blow up If you get your social media game on point. Social media is all down to the right techniques, execution and reachability. Social media marketing has proven to change the face of many failing businesses, so not using it would be professional suicide.

Social media has proven time and time again that it will only get bigger and better, this internet phenomenon is only growing so you should really start investing your time and energy into learning social media marketing.
Be bold and be different!

CONTENT TIP:

———— MODIFY MEDIA TOP TIPS ————
Republish old content. There's no reason not to shout about good stuff you've done in the past, reposting previous work is absolutely fine just do not over do it.

Facebook

Facebook by far is the most successful social media application to date, with an estimated two billion active monthly users. Over 60% of Facebooks active users, log in every day. Now with that in mind imagine you had a product or service of which you wanted to share, it would seem Facebook would be the perfect platform to access a vast amount of potential customers.

Around 70% of small/local businesses utilise the power of social media, which also suggests that your closest competition already has a Facebook page.

Before you leap ahead with sharing your product or service, you may want to look at how Facebook works for business. Facebook has a good amount of advertising campaigns and strategies available for its business users, of which if done correctly could really boost your business to unimaginable success.

We've heard it before, where someone has gone viral overnight and created massive profits in sales through a well planned out Facebook ad campaign. Although this massive success can happen in short periods, bare in mind its the long game you want to be playing for.

By a long game we mean keeping up with regular posts, of which will increase interactions regularly and grow your social media audience.

Think compound affect, to which you adapt to your social media platform and you've got it! Consistent, quality content will always prevail online, especially if your brand is engaging and building relationships along the way.

SNAPCHAT / LIVE VIDEO TIP:

—— MODIFY MEDIA TOP TIPS ——

Behind-the-scenes photos: Take exclusive shots of yourself, your employees, or a shot of your office or workspace. This should give your viewers a feeling of connectivity.

Facebook for business

Firstly if you actually just visit (https://www.facebook.com/business) there are some great hints, tips and demonstrations on how to maximise your Facebook business page to its potential. Bare in mind Facebook do want you to pay for boosted posts aka adverts. So much of Facebooks communication with you will be suggestions on 'boosting posts'.
(We look at content marketing later to save you money on advertising)

Facebook have some great quick and easy to use features to create posts, many of which you can get direct calls, direct messages, add links to external websites, even add videos to these advertising posts if you wish.
We highly suggest images and videos on Facebook adverts, as adverts with a visual affect generate around 80% more of a response rate then just boosted posts with a lot of wording.

Remember getting likes and followers is great, but creating sales, increasing engagement and growing your brand is always better then growing your ego.
Many businesses boast about how they have over 10,000 likes on their business page, this is no representation to their content, brand and especially no reflection on the amount of customers or clients that are actually using their product or services.

A statistic once stated that 95% of followers wall posts to business pages are not answered, this is

a great way to let your business stand out. Reply to your followers.
Become apart of the interaction and get stuck in online, this will help build trust and relationships.

Always try and add CTA's (Call to action) onto your Facebook adverts or posts, this will help turn interested individuals into paying customers.

TIME SAVING TIP:

MODIFY MEDIA TOP TIPS

Schedule your posts on social media for evenings and weekends so you don't miss out on good traffic. This will also save you time later, if you find you are short of time to get online.

Whats best for business a page or group?

Its common knowledge that starting a Facebook page is fairly easy for most, it is also common knowledge that individuals rarely weigh up the options of which type of page or possibly a group they should choose for their business.
Setting up a business page for your business is common sense, so why would you need to think about anything else?..

The question here is, what is better?
Should you have a business page and should you have a group linked to the page?
What will help you and your business reach your desired goals?

We get into some more detail below for you, but for now lets assume you know a Facebook Page is simply a profile page dedicated to businesses, brands, celebrities, and organisations.

If you search on Facebook in your local area you will see 'Buy, Sell, Swap' groups, which have thousands of local people all buying and selling a lot of the time. These groups are very community based, where people interact with each others posts, often meeting up buying items from each other.

Other groups have been set up where many people interact over the same interests, such as gym groups, or healthy eating groups. These Facebook groups form their own community feel.

Facebook groups

Facebook groups are more collective and collaborative in nature, with many being interactive for all the members.

Groups can be set up for a vast number of reasons such as common interests, support groups, even groups for businesses for more of a connection with your customers.

Groups can now be set up and added to a business page, of which the business page can post within the group as a page.
A group added to a business page is big news! This gives your page a opportunity to post in a group and become more interactive with your clients and customers.

Facebook groups are especially important, as they give you the opportunity to become more personal and more direct as a business with your customers.
A group along with your business page, helps you stay more interactive within your business community.

A great aspect of Facebook groups is the ability to add members to your group, of which they will automatically be added.
Where as with Facebook pages you invite friends to like your page, of which many decide not to support your business page and will not like your page..

Sad truth of how little support is shown by family and friends.

A Facebook group also gives you the ability to sell products within your group, which can also be posted in your group by your linked business page. Groups also have added extras such as interactive polls, add files and more
Groups can have a more personal yet privet feel for your clients or customers, the settings of a group can also be set as:

Public
Anyone can see the group, its members and their posts.

Closed
Anyone can find the group and see who's in it. Only members can see posts.

Secret
Only members can find the group and see posts.

Facebook groups also give you the option to add additional group admins who can help you run a group, should you feel the need to give someone else some authority within your group.
This is much like various admins on a business page.

Groups can be limited to only show a admins post, this would mean individuals within your group will not be able to create posts, but will be able to interact with your posts.
A added option is allowing individuals within your group to create posts of their own, this could be useful if you was to use this group as a way of customer relations and feedback.

QUICK LOOK AT GROUPS

- Members can engage in group chats.

- Members can post text files to share and search within group conversations.

- Facebook groups give a community feeling among members.

- Members are more likely to give access to their friends, rather then suggest their friends like a page.
  (Only if your group is full of value and appealing)

- As a business you can create a more exclusive feeling by giving group members special discounts and offers.

FACEBOOK TIP:

―――― MODIFY MEDIA TOP TIPS ――――
Don't hard sell. This is very important. People are not generally looking to buy on Facebook. Show them something genuinely interesting, which will increase the chances of engagement..

Group tips:

- When you first open your group leave it public, so people can get a feel and idea of what your group is about, this will help Increase some interest to start your group off. At a later date turn your group privet, for a more exclusive feel for your customers/clients.

- Your banner/header should be branded the same or similar to your business, or Facebook business page. This will help those relate all your platforms back to your brand.

- Start a hashtag within your group of which should be added to your banner. A hashtag once built moment will help your brand strength and exposure for prospective customers.

- If your group generates a large member count, it would be wise to connect with your most active members to help track the group, acting as your spam police to stop unwanted comments or behaviour.

- Start a engaging activity such as 'Motivation Monday', where members can post there motivational inspiring posts, videos, quotes, etc. You can also do other variants such as 'Selfie Saturdays', or 'Fired up Fridays'. These special occasions will help initiate conversation between members, to which you can also participate in this interaction.

- You can do Live Q&A's to help boost engagement within your group, Facebook algorithms love live videos and notify your members/followers when you do a live video on your page, profile, or group.

CONTENT TIP:

Post a link to an old blog post: There's nothing wrong with recycling, and old posts will gain new engagement, extending their life. This is all apart of your reditributio

Facebook pages

A Facebook page in simple terms is a profile page dedicated to your business, there are other options such as brands, celebrity and organisations.
Creating a page is fairly straight forward, you create a page and then start sharing your link to friends, family and customers/clients.

Sharing your Facebook page usually goes a little like this: Find us at @MODIFYMEDIA

The great thing about a Facebook page is the fact that you are able to add the Facebook logo to a lot of your other offline PR and advertising campaigns.
You will notice many businesses have the Facebook logo on vans, flyers, business cards, etc.

One thing you will notice straight away when you create your Facebook page is the lack of friends and family that actually support your business. Facebook gives you notifications of which you will see the interactions on your page, these notifications and analytics display interactions from your supporters, customers and random engagements.

Facebook analytics

You will be able to track
which posts are performing
well, also which campaigns
attract a larger engagement
response.
The analytics on Facebook
pages are the perfect tool,
of which will help you target your desired
demographic and grow your Facebook page.

Paying for advertising on Facebook is very simple,
it is literally just a few clicks away when 'boosting
posts'.
In other cases you can post a attractive video
advert, to match nice in depth wording of which
will explain the product/service.
You can also add a excellent call to action, which
can lead straight to a landing page of some sort.
Your call to action could even direct them to make
contact straight away.

Another option is to create such a advert that is
set up to help capture emails through a couple
clicks, this would all be part of your email
marketing strategy
(More on email marketing later).

Facebook advertising and analytics should be
your deciding factor to create a Facebook page,
as the analytics alone are one of your greatest
tools when creating content and viewing how
people engaged with your content. You can use
these analytics to improve your marketing
strategies, but there is more, much more.

Facebook Verification

The great thing about creating a Facebook page is
you appear more certified as a trusted business. It
has come to a age where your business is
questioned, if it does not have any
social media profiles.

Once you have proven who you are,
your business has been set up on
Facebook, then you can actually really
get your business certified.
A great aspect of becoming certified on Facebook
is your page will rank higher in relevant searches.

A certified business lets customers know that
you've taken the time to contact Facebook and
supply the right information to get either a grey
certified tick, or for larger businesses, celebrities,
brands and influencers it will be a blue certified
tick.

The main issue many have is choosing the right page to create, below are your choices:

- Local business or Place
- Company, Organisation or Institute
- Brand or Product
- Artist, Band or Public figure
- Entertainment
- Cause or Community

Once you have selected one of these options, you will then get another more specific category to choose from. Although this may seem a bit technical, there are many advantages or disadvantage to each choice.

For local everyday small to medium size businesses, looking to expand online and within their local area.
We suggest choosing 'Local business or Place'. When you choose this option and your page is set up you will then get the options to sell products through links, offer services with prices and individuals can also 'check in' at your business.

Checking in to a place of business is a big deal, as this feature lets you show up on your clients and customers posts when they 'check in'.
When you show up on their posts, this allows their friends and family see your place of business, this is great news for you if their posts are positive posts or pictures.

Checking in will also allow you to see who and when someone visited your place of business. The checking in data will be useful in the future when you want to analysis who has interacted with your place of business.

Having a page where people can check in helps your page be found much easier, this allows others to search and find you very easy.

ENGAGMENT TIP:

—◄— MODIFY MEDIA TOP TIPS —►—

Questions: Pose simple, basic questions that your followers can answer quickly. Quick easy to answer questions will increase your chances of engagement.

QUICK LOOK AT FACEBOOK PAGES

• As a business page you will appear more certified, of which people will install more trust into your business or brand.

• On a Facebook page you can get access to the information about performance, including user demographic data. Facebook analytics and data is the perfect tool for your growth on the platform, this reason alone is enough to create a Facebook business page.
You can see the data through the 'page insights' section.

• Businesses can create CTA's on the page through various post options, calls to actions will help to drive your business towards it's desired goals.
CTA = Call to action.

• As a page you have the added option to schedule posts to appear at the desired time, this is really useful if you have a busy schedule or want to optimise your posts to suit the busiest time's on your page.

• Facebook pages show up in google searches, so this will give you the added reachability and exposure to be located easier. Increasing your exposure to a possible 2 billion+ Facebook users..

- Starting a Facebook business page costs £0, but the returns on your reachability is enormous. You will have the option to share and create content, affectively advertising without costing you a lot of money. (Content marketing - Coming up in this book)

CONTENT TIP:

MODIFY MEDIA TOP TIPS

Post a branded or watermarked image: Posting a funny or inspirational image with your logo or website URL on it, could gain you more traction from that images reach. If that image is shared elsewhere, then your brand will follow.

Facebook Footprints

Facebook footprints are your digital footprint on another profile or page. Once you have created a Facebook page for your business, you then have the opportunity to comment, share and engage with others on Facebook through your page.

A great quality of networking through your Facebook page is the fact that other businesses, brands and celebrities will become aware of your business page. The added bonus of these digital footprints are, not only do the pages your interacting with become aware of your interactions but also their followers become aware of your interactions.

You can share and tag other brands, celebrities, or businesses content through your page, if you are to share other peoples content its always good practice to tag the original creator in their content. Tagging the original creator of content allows them to see who is sharing their content, it also shows that you are not trying to take credit for content you did not create.

The added bonus of sharing others content, is you have been able to re-distribute others content with your followers, which also lets you update your platforms more regularly keeping your followers engaged with you.

Please check a example of Facebook footprints in the image below.

Face Down Musik
Published by Patrick Long [?] · 7 mins · ⊙

Contact us to share your talents!🎵

Example B shows how you can change the option to comment as your page rather then commenting as a personal profile, this will then lead you to **Example A** of which shows how you can leave that digital footprint as your page.

You can clearly see from the image that we have left a comment and liked the original status all through our page. The reason for this interaction is simply to network with those in our industry, networking with those in your industry is a great way to build relationships and become a leader within that industry.

Another reason to network and leave digital footprints is to allow their followers see who you are through these interactions. These digital footprints will be left on others content indefinitely, this means at any point your digital footprint can be discovered and spark interest with a new follower.

ADVERTISINGTIP:

MODIFY MEDIA TOP TIPS

YES! Advertising on social media is in many cases a waste of money if not done correctly.

You must learn content marketing to be able to maximise the effect and reach of your posts. Once you master creating quality posts, then adding additional boosts or paid promotions will really help you excel on social media.

Facebook advertising

Over two billion people use Facebook every month, with a staggering one out of every five minutes spent on a mobile, is on Facebook. Learning how to advertise on Facebook could be very profitable if done correctly.

Most people start a Facebook page, invite all their friends to like the page, once this is done they can start sharing loads of offers or creating sales posts..... STOP!

This method alone will destroy your business on social media, whilst weakening your brand.

Applying content marketing and providing valuable posts will increase your chances of becoming successful through Facebook ads.
Your everyday posts, your content, your paid posts, your boosted post all represent your business, remember this when you do want to sell.

This is all well and good, but what about really good deals, surly everyone will see these posts and snap them up!?..

True, if a really good boosted posts or Facebook adverts are created then yes people will buy from you.
Although you still need to target the right people with these fantastic offers, so how can you do that?

As you can see in the image below trial and error is all apart of your learning process on social media.

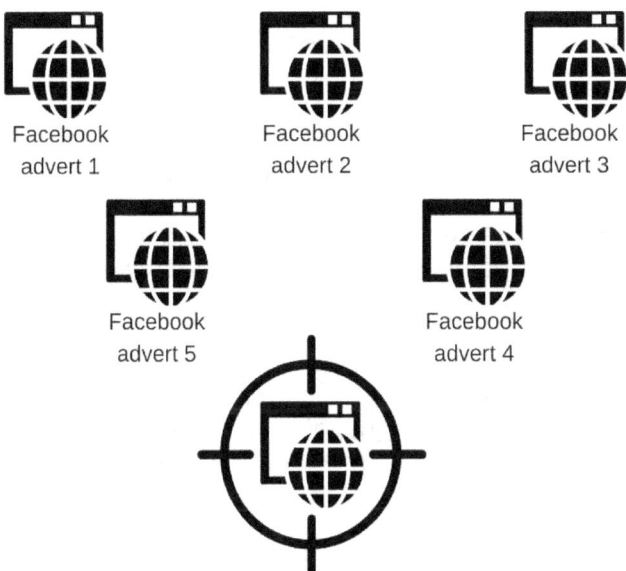

Filter through your adverts to fine tune where your target market is, this way you will have a better idea of your demographic through trial and error testing.

For example if you have £1000 to spend on social media advertising, its a good idea to test a couple of similar adverts to see which settings or demographics react best.
This way you do not blow the full advertising budget on one advert, with limited results.

You may have 3 adverts (one to three above) running at £100 each and showing some results, of which you can then take these results further.

The next set of adverts you run which will be adverts four and five above, will be more targeted to the demographics you haver found to react best from your first 3 campaigns.
These adverts you can also run at £100 each, but should produce a lot better results then your first three advertising campaigns.

After some testing you will know exactly which demographics work best and which settings to apply on each advert.
This trial and error period is a really good way to test your potential audience and attract potential customers.

Finally once you have found out what works best you can start using this information for £500 advertising campaigns, of which should produce fantastic results due to your rigorous testing methods.

ADVERTISINGTIP:

Test and measure what combination of images, videos, campaigns and adverts work best for your target market. Keeping track of past results, will increase future progress.

Facebook spamming is bad news, but it works..

When most people start out in business and they get online they start sharing their links, or their content with friends and family. It is normal to want to share your business with the people you know online, but sometimes individuals do go to far.

Spam or spamming is sending the same message/content to a large number of internet users, some times repeating this process to the same users.
It is fair to say we all would love to go viral, or attract a lot of attention to lead to massive boosts within our businesses. Spam or spamming is not the way to do it.
Facebook frown on this sort of behaviour and if caught you face harsh but fair punishment from the Facebook police.

If you are caught over spamming by sharing the same link/content to much and they deem this to be a case of spamming, then you face having your account frozen from sharing your content.
Having your account frozen from sharing means no more posting, you can still talk and interact with others but no more posting content of your own on Facebook.
You may have a week long ban on sharing in groups, you may even have a suspended account until you resolve your case with Facebook.

Either way you look at it, getting caught spamming is not the way you want to go when expressing your business on Facebook. You will essentially be weakening your brand by over spamming and annoying fellow Facebook users.

Although we do suggest redistribution of older valuable content, we do not suggest you over do it.

You may be thinking 'How can they say yes share links, but do not over share links?'
Here are frequent questions and answers for you:

At what point is it over sharing?

Only you can decide this, but a good indication is the amount of time your spending sharing your content, rather then making fresh new content.
If you find yourself thinking about sharing content to much, then you should take a break and start thinking about creating new, fresh, valuable content.
Simply a small amount of sharing is good for you, whilst over sharing is spamming.
You should be spending more time planning and creating fresh content then you do sharing older content.

Where do you share your posts or your content?

Once you have created your posts, you may want to share that post to maximise reach. The obvious way to maximise your reach on your quality post would be to pay to boost/advertise your post.
A few other examples may be:

• Sharing in groups within your industry.

- Sharing on friends and families personal profiles, with permission.

- Posting your content on your personal profile, of which you may also want to tag friends and family.

- Sharing your posts in others pages comment boxes, or directly on other pages is not ideal as many pages do not like their comments filled with people trying to steal their followers. Although interacting with others content in their comments box is a part of networking and becoming a part of that content they have created.

We suggest if you are going to be tagging friends and family check with them first, also posting on their walls can become a nuisance so make sure to just check they are ok with a few posts. The last thing you want to do is annoy those on your personal profile as these are the people most likely to ask you about the work you do.
A idea would be to get people on your Facebook involved in your content, so when you do tag them or share with them they are happy to re-share even further among their friends.

For example:

A personal trainer may invite a group of 3 friends down for a free filmed personal training session, or Facebook live personal training session. Tagging them in this content will raise the chances of them re-sharing and also increase the chances of their friends engaging in the content.

Posting within groups is one of the main ways many share their content for free on Facebook, but it has limited engagement as so many people are doing this. You can share in groups as much as you like until you are caught spamming and being a nuisance, or you can share different content in groups every other day so that you do not over redistribute the same content.

NETWORKING TIP:

MODIFY MEDIA TOP TIPS

Find influencers and ask them to share your content.
Finding and connecting with influencers is hard to do,
without sounding like you want them to advertise for
you. Be genuine and create relationships.

Creating a quality Facebook post

You may think that Facebook posts are simple, as in you put a image up and then wait for people to like it. Perhaps you decide you will run a new offer on your Facebook page, which will be a image and a description saying '30% off this week'.

You are right to assume this is advertising on Facebook, the only downside is the sheer laziness within the majority of the posts businesses are offering their followers.
DO NOT always post offers, services and products on Facebook, as it becomes boring.
If you want to attract customers, then your posts need to be attractive. You will need to learn content marketing, of which you will later in this book.

Your Facebook page needs to be appealing, engaging and worth clicking on.
Offer some free informative posts, or try some entertaining material of which your followers will enjoy.
Get stuck in engaging with your followers on your posts and become a brand they can connect with.
All of this would be the value you are creating for your following, of which is 'content marketing'.

Do not forget people initially didn't come on Facebook to be sold to, so don't be the page they skip past because you are always selling.
People are on Facebook to connect, to browse, to be entertained, to find something of interest and lastly to be social.

ADVERTISINGTIP:

MODIFY MEDIA TOP TIPS

LIKE · SHARE · COMMENT · TAG

This simple method of running a competition to increase engagement with your post, they like, share, comment and tag people on your image or video and at the end of the competition you choose a lucky winner.
This is done by many businesses, this competition can get a large amount of engagement if the prize is good enough.

Below is a example of a good quality post that will increase your chances of engagement on Facebook:

QUESTIONS WITHIN YOUR POSTS INCREASE ENGAGEMENT. BULLET POINTS AND SIMPLE INFORMATION PERFORM BEST.

MODIFY MEDIA
Just now

Looking for support with your social media platforms?

Look no further then MODIFY MEDIA. We specialise in social media marketing and content creation, to help businesses become more successful online.

• Content creation... See More

ALWAYS ADD A IMAGE OR VIDEO TO YOUR POSTS. IMAGES GET OVER 50% MORE ENGAGEMENT. VIDEOS GET OVER 70% MORE ENGAGEMENT.

Full video production
Photography services
Content creation techniques
Social media marketing specialists

MODIFY MEDIA

Modify Media is a multi-platform media company, covering all aspects of business boosting strategies. Contact us today! For a free phone consultation!

Send Message

ADD A CALL TO ACTION BUTTON ON YOUR POSTS

Top tips for a quality post on Facebook:

- Ask a question, but be direct. Being direct will result in a easy choice of answers boosting your chances of engagement.

- Keep it short and sweet, by doing this you give people the opportunity of skimming their Facebook feed and noticing your post.

- Give a clear Call-To-Action. Dumb it down a little, its not that people are dumb but always remember (k.i.s.s = keep it simple stupid) the simpler the request the greater chance of a positive result.

- Offer some valuable information, just enough to entice them to take action. Your main aim is to interest people enough for them to engage with your post and click on your call to action.

- Always add a image or video content to your posts. As stated you will get over 50% more engagement for images and over 70% more engagement through video content. Get creative with your post and learn to stand out with your visual content.

ENGAGEMENT TIP:

MODIFY MEDIA TOP TIPS

Encourage conversation and increase engagement, by asking people questions.

FACEBOOK tasks & notes..

What groups have you joined to become apart of your industry or niche?
(In these groups you will also be able to redistribute your valuable quality content, but do not spam)

Which pages in your industry have you actively started commenting on, as your page?
(Do not spam, but do get stuck into the conversations going on in the comments through your page)

Have you started a linked Facebook group yet, if so have you started a 'motivation Monday' or 'selfie Saturday' to increase engagement within your group?

Whilst inviting all your friends and family to like your Facebook page, have you sent them a personal message with the same invite?
(This is a option on your page, when you invite new people)

Have you contacted Facebook with the right documentation, to try and get your Facebook page verified?
(Verified pages rank higher in relevant searches)

Have you tried a variety of smaller Facebook adverts to test the demographic?
(After some testing is done with your target market, you will then be able to advertise more effectively in the future)

NOTES:

Twitter

Send me a tweet. If you are familiar to twitter you will know exactly what this means, but if you are not actively tweeting then this will sound like a very bad slang word for some sort of communication.

Tweeting was once called micro-blogging in the beginning, but although this is one of the most simple social media platforms to use it is also very limited.
280 characters is all you can have in each tweet, of which lets twitter stand out from the crowed of social media giants. A tweet is your status or micro-blog, its your broadcast to the world aka people who see your tweets. The better the tweet, the better the chances of a retweet and the message, image or short video will reach further.

Perhaps long drawn out Facebook statuses annoy you, or endless pictures and videos bore you. Then twitter is your place to be, as twitter limited the images to only 4 per tweet and videos can only be 140 seconds long. This limitation lets twitter stand out, whilst also keeping things short and sweet.

Some suggest that twitter is dying out, but in all honesty it has still been able to hold its ground among the social media giants of today.
Maybe its the cool way twitter doesn't overflow you with endless amounts of images and video, or long statuses.

Maybe its the fact that people have taken time to build up a following on this social media platform, of which enriches their hold onto twitter. No one wants to invest time and effort to lose their social media account especially if that account holds a large following.

If you do decide to jump into twitter and start tweeting, then remember keep it short, sweet and really engage with those who engage with you. Building relationships on twitter is great way to get re-tweets and support others in your industry.

Twitter is also a great place to connect to brands, businesses, celebrities and influencers.
Twitter is by far one of the easiest methods of a little communications with these examples, as many celebrities and big brands often retweet their fans, or followers.

Twitter has recently jumped on the live video bandwagon, with the rest of the social media world so thats great to keep in mind. Remember most social media algorithms love a good live video.

So make sure if you do get into tweeting and connecting with the world through twitter, you should utilise the live video feature.
If you are on Twitter, Instagram and Facebook you can do a full live broadcast through all three at the same time. This idea is done by many social media entrepreneurs.

To do such live video and broadcast through all three platforms you will need the relevant devices to do so, but take a look at Tai Lopez on social media. Tai Lopez leverages the power of multiple platforms including Twitter, so he may be someone you can take some notes from in regards to business and social media usage.

Twitter is renowned for its hash tagging, but it is used more on Instagram where people flood their content with hashtags. Twitter is more select and focused, to a point many news stations search twitter hashtags to look for related news stories or updates.

Twitter users   are advised not to flood their tweets with multiple hashtags, the best practice is around two hashtags per post.
Hash tagging was once referred to as 'Twitter groupings', but we do not need to explain hashtags any more.

NETWORKING TIP:

—————— MODIFY MEDIA TOP TIPS ——————

Share other people's content. Make sure to keep it relevant to your industry and interesting.

Below is a example of a good quality tweet:

A short and sweet description is key to twitter. Be sure to tag anyone in the content description who is involved in the post.
Tweets under 100 characters, gain 21% increase in interaction.

It is advised that you use no more then two hashtags for best results.

Images are key to success on twitter, as 80% of twitter users are accessing the site via mobile. Short sweet descriptions and clear images increase chances of engagement. Be sure to tag anyone else who is in the image or apart of the content being posted.

As with all social media platforms relating to businesses, who want to be found, you should tag your location.

Tweet

MODIFY MEDIA
@ModifyMedia

Modify Media Tip!

Here is a hot tip on content sharing and networking.

#Networking #SocialMediaTip

NETWORKING TIP:

MODIFY MEDIA TOP TIPS

Share other people's content. Make sure to keep it relevant to your industry and interesting.

a MODIFYMEDIA

MODIFY MEDIA

You
15/09/2017, 13:31 from Eastbourne, England

TOP TIPS FOR TWITTER SUCCESS:

- Images - Peoples interact twice as much with images on twitter, so make sure you utilise the power of images when you are tweeting

- Connecting with leaders - Twitter is a great place to interact with celebrities, brands, businesses and influencers. Be sure that you are reaching out and building relationships with the leading authorities on twitter.

- Short and sweet - Keeping your tweets short and sweet is vital on twitter, thats why they only allow 280 characters.
  Twitter posts with under 100 characters gain a 21% increase in interaction on twitter.

- Trending with hashtags aka 'News jacking' - Jumping on a trending hashtag is a great way to increase your chances of being noticed on twitter. When a hashtag is trending and you use it within your tweets, others will search for and find your content. Try and relate to the hashtag you have used and not just use it for no reason. Getting onboard with hash tag trending is a example of news jacking, of which you will see more of in the content marketing section in this book.

- Timing - As with much of internet use and social media usage, there are certain times of which is best to post or in this case tweet. According to studies, twitter posts have a relatively short life span of roughly 30 minutes. Your prime time to

post on twitter is recorded to be around 3pm Monday to Friday.
This may vary depending on your audience, location and content strategy.

- BTS aka behind the scenes - Using twitter for what it was made for, short and quick updates is great. What if all of these short and quick updates, actually showed behind the scenes of the longer more in depth content being created for YouTube, or Facebook. You could give your twitter followers exclusive back stage access to you and your business. A feeling of never before seen footage and quick intros to increase interest to your other platforms.

- Give credit - When you find something of value online then give it a tweet, share that content with your following. When you share others content be sure to tag them or give them credit for the content they have created. Giving credit or shoutouts builds relationships online, of which shares followers when people are crossposting each others content. Make sure to follow those in your industry, to stay unto date with their tweets.

- Get involved - If you see a hot tweet getting a lot of attention within your industry, then make sure you get stuck in tweeting your opinion and ideas. Although it may not be your original tweet, becoming apart of the conversation will get you noticed by others and respected if your point of view or tweets are relevant and insightful. Becoming apart of your marketplace on social media, means becoming more social and engaging with other people.

Twitter tasks & notes..

What two hash tags will you apply to each post on twitter?
(Studies suggest twitter posts with two hash tags get higher engagement, then those with more then two hash tags)

Do you have your twitter account linked to your Facebook and Instagram accounts?
(Linked accounts helps with cross posting)

Have you chosen some industry leaders, influencers, or celebrities you will continually interact with through twitter?
(Twitter is a great platform for engaging with industry leaders, influencers and celebrities)

NOTES:

YouTube

YouTube is the number one website people use all the time for 'How to' videos. Its fairly straight forward if your looking for something online you start with a quick search on google, of which does display YouTube links to match the content you are searching for on google.
Google actually own YouTube so its no surprise they work together to bring you the best possible results for your search.

YouTube was created by three former PayPal employees back in 2005, of which it was originally intended for people to post and share original content. Since then YouTube has become the number one video sharing platform for businesses, artist, new movie trailers, new product lunches and so much more!

YouTube is a endless supply of video content, you just get online and start watching. Remember the simplicity of watching one video, then the next, then another, this could go on forever....
YouTube is addictive just like any other social media platform and people literally lose hours every day from watching YouTube videos. People spend hours watching, learning and being entertained by the channels they love.

If someone likes washing cars, then you can guarantee there is a channel somewhere out there for car washing tips, tricks and how to's.
Actually there is and these videos are getting millions of views, with quality feedback.

So the big question should be, why are you not on YouTube?
Wouldn't you want to be one of the channels capturing your potential customers attention?
You can pick up a camera and start today, just create some quality content and start sharing your expertise with the world. There will be people who will learn, enjoy and share your content if it is of value to them.

Did you know over 300 hours of video is uploaded every single day on YouTube. With this amount of content being uploaded to a platform, some businesses may question if this if this is a viable market place for their business.

Although that is a astonishing amount of content being uploaded every single day, YouTube is still easier to rank higher then google. If you want to be found, then you must be considering YouTube, additionally as a extra means of being discovered. This means if you are trying to get noticed online, then getting your website, or blog site up to SEO scratch is all well and good, but YouTube may help increase your chances of being found.

You best start thinking about some top quality videos to release, as YouTube is only growing. Video content returns a much higher response rate on all social media platforms not just YouTube, so be a little creative and start thinking about video production for you and your business.

The term 'viral video' is a exciting term for business owners. As we stated earlier in the book, viral content could really propel your business and sales to unimaginable heights over night. Although gaining massive sales from viral content is not the easiest thing to do, it doesn't stop it being of excitement to business owners and entrepreneurs alike.

FACEBOOK TIP:

MODIFY MEDIA TOP TIPS

Post directly to Facebook rather than using a social media management platforms like Hootsuite or Buffer. Facebook's algorithms prefer content that is published directly.

How to create a YouTube video, our tips for beginners. (Smart phone filming)

Firstly lets get this fantasy that you need a huge budget and a great production team behind you. A good camera and quality microphone is a great start to your new venture on YouTube, but lets assume you don't have a nice camera, or sound equipment.

All you really need is your smart phone to start, some internet access and little creativity. Thats all you need to get started on YouTube, literally that is all.

So many fall into the mindset that they cant get started on YouTube because they do not own a video camera, they don't have the right lighting, or the editing skills and so on.

Did you no a large majority of big Youtube names all started or still use their mobile device for filming, especially the Vlogs (Video diary). Those who are busy creating content, are not sitting around thinking they will never be good enough..

Start creating content today, by using what you have, where you are and learn along the way. Improve and upgrade your video making process as you progress, it is a fantastic piece of advice we should all take onboard.

Most mobile phones have exceptionally good cameras now days, of which we did not have many years ago.

Whilst mobile devices are great, investing in a good camera and quality microphone will substantially improve your video quality at a later date. For now lets assume you just have your mobile device.

We have advanced so much in mobile device technology, that many believe all you need is a smart phone.

No cameras, no laptops, no computers and no being tied down to your wifi location. Although all these do help with production and presentation, they are not essential.

Some believe that all you need is a smart phone, some internet access and your ready to create some video magic, but that all said, lets assume you are not that creative.

INSTAGRAM TIP:

TOP TIPS for YouTube filming..

- Planning - Although catching live videos, or random videos around your business is great video content for your customers. It is also a great idea to plan videos in advance, so your video runs smoothly on the day of filming. This will help the video quality appear more professional for your followers.

- Lighting - Assuming your very new to this we suggest well light and vibrant areas for filming, as this will help the appearance of the overall production. A well lite area also shows a friendly approachable business, of which will attract more customers.

- Using your smart phone - Ok you can live stream from a smart phone on various social media platforms, but we are now talking about a YouTube video production. Always film with your phone 'Landscape', as this gets a full image rather then filming 'portrait' of which cuts off the sides when you use the video footage anywhere. Filming Portrait will leave black lines or marks when you post the footage online, this is not a good look for a YouTube video.

- Filming - Hold the smart phone with both hands if you don't have a phone holder, or small tripod. Keeping footage steady also adds value to your video production, there is nothing worse then shaky, unclear footage out of focus. That being said people will understand if you are filming a vlog, or behind the scenes type footage of your business.

- Apps for edits - Video editing can be big business and costly, also confusing if you are not technology savvy. You can now download very simple apps to help place some very basic bits to your videos you have filmed.
These apps can add multiple videos together, add music, wording and more.
Take a look and trial some video editing apps on your smart phone. Wording on videos is a big deal as many individuals online rarely click to listen to the sound of a video, especially if they are scrolling on social media.

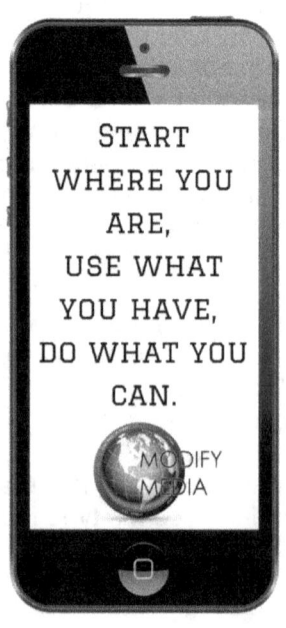

START
WHERE YOU
ARE,
USE WHAT
YOU HAVE,
DO WHAT YOU
CAN.

MODIFY
MEDIA

How to upload your video, to increase your chances of ranking higher in searches.

Once you have filmed, edited and created the desired YouTube video the way you want it. You now will need to upload it to YouTube.

The one thing many fail at when it comes to social media is the way the content is present, or how they post their content. Certain ways of posting a piece of content will attract a higher view rate, or larger engagement. Keep in mind your meta data and how meta data affects your content online.

1. Title

For example lets say your a florist and you have taken the time out to create a lovely video showing how to present and prepare your flowers once you get home from a florist.
Uploading your video and adding the title 'Flowers at home' is unlikely to get many views on YouTube. The title has to be something that people will search for, your title is your first key aspect to increasing your view count.

For example lets say you now retitle this video for your florist business. Lets say you now title the video 'How to present your flowers at home'. This title alone has your first title in it, whilst also containing 'How to'.
As we are fully aware 'How to' and 'What is' are big for youtube and google. So trying to link your

video to these will help boost its chances of being searched for. A fantastic title is not all you need to be able to maximise your reach..

2. Description

A title is just the start of the process to increasing your reach. Underneath your title you have the option for a description to go with your video. A well written and well planned out description is key for those who want to help engage with the viewers.
Adding a description to your video will allow viewers to know and learn more about your video.

Descriptions help your video stand out, especially if your description has some quality information for your viewers. Even in the description box it is always good practice to continue to give value to your viewers. Remember if your video is of value to your viewer, then they may want to see more of you, which will increase their chances of subscribing to your channel.

Adding your website is common amongst many who create YouTube videos, but just your website link alone may scare or bore your viewers.
A great link to add into your description is a link to another one of your YouTube videos. Adding a link to another video, helps YouTube retain viewers of which the video sharing platform love!
Also another great reason to add another video link in your description, is to help you up your view count and bring more value to your viewers.

YouTube will give you 5000 characters to use in your description field, but the first couple of sentences are key to maximising your reachability. YouTube and Google use your first few sentences and key words as part of the meta data.

This meaning that a good amount of keywords will be picked up and help you be noticed online, also the first line or two will appear on external searches. Your first few lines pop up to explain the video, along with your thumbnail image in google searches.

3. Tags

Tags is the last port of call underneath the loading of your fantastic video to YouTube.
(There are other options we will discuss, but for now just the title, description and tags)

Your tags section is pretty straight forward its YouTube's way of adding hashtag's to its content. The tag section is your time to shine with your key words for that video, but remember it is not Instagram so don't fill it with a whole lot of one word tags for extra reach.
That just wont work on YouTube, the algorithms are different for each social media platform.

Firstly when it comes to tagging your content on YouTube, you will want to add variations of your brand-specific tags.
Remember when we spoke about hashtags earlier in this book and said it is a good idea to create your own hashtag relating back to your brand or business.

For example we would add the tag Modify Media, but it is good practice to add variations of this to increase the chances of people finding your content relating to your brand.
A example would be:
ModifyMedia
Modify Media
modifymedia.net

Also other similar tags all relating back to your business, this will help your content pop up when someone searches for your business.
One of the best ways to add a good tag into the tag section on YouTube, is with YouTubes auto-suggest option.
What we mean by auto-suggest is playing with the search bar and see what similar videos are being called and searched for.
You may be looking at creating a video for tips on washing a car, so simply type in what you believe other people would be searching for.

When you have a idea of others searches and how many search results are found for similar videos, then it will be easier to create your own tag and possible very similar to their tag/title. The reason we do this is when the tags/titles are searched for, then it is likely that your video will pop up.

Whilst we are on the subject of searching for other peoples similar content, never try to replicate their tags and titles to the exact word. You will be lost behind their video and other creators videos who have copied their content.
You will want to be similar but not the same, add a genuine touch to your content of which others will respect and appreciate as you grow.

This is how your video will appear on a Google search

SO Fit personal training promotion video, produced by Modify Media ...

 https://www.youtube.com/watch?v=Ct6xcf2iVLU
15 Jun 2017 - Uploaded by Modify Media
Here is a video freshly produced for SO Fit Personal Training based in East
Sussex. This video was produced ...

⇧

Your thumbnail is very important, it is the key factor of which someone will decide to click and play the video or not.

↖

The first few lines of your description is very important and should relate to your title with keywords.
The reason we use keywords and a informative description, is the fact that external sources such as Google use these as meta data in online searches. Increasing your chances of being found online is key to increasing your reachability, all from the wording around your YouTube content.

SNAPCHAT TIP:

Be a human on snapchat. This is not the platform on which to talk about 'Business, marketing techniques and non stop product drives'. Create some entertaining or engaging content for your snapchat followers to enjoy.

Top tips for YouTube

- Your network = Your net worth - Ok your network does not actually equal your net worth, but the saying does hold some value to it.
Collaborating online on any social media platform is always good practice, especially with YouTube.
Another YouTuber may have similar interest, or content of which both parties can benefit from a collaboration video.
YouTube is especially good to collaborate on as YouTube is one of the hardest social media platforms to become successful on, with support from others online the task will be easier to accomplish. Cross networking your followers is key to a faster growing YouTube channel.

- Consistency is key - The saying content is king is very true online, but consistent content is key to retaining your viewers and followers. It's all well and good creating a fantastic piece of valuable content that gets a lot of engagement, whilst boosting your audience.
Remember, if your audience hasn't got something to watch next week then they are likely to start to slowly unsubscribe. Content is king, but consistency will keep your audience engaged and interacting with your growth on YouTube.

- Make it attractive - The main aim of your video is to attract views, to attract attention of which will increase subscribers and followers that lead to a increase in engagement.
The first thing people will see is the eye catching

thumbnail you have displayed to draw their attention to your video. Your eye catching thumbnail will be paired with a enticing title to get more clicks.

• Engage for engagement - With all social media platforms, one of the best ways to increase engagement and reachability, is to get stuck in yourself.
Reach out on to other peoples channels and get stuck in with the conversation, especially the conversations and content relating to your industry.
Remember when we spoke about 'Facebook footprints', well this is the same thing. Getting involved in conversations and leaving comments is your digital footprint on YouTube.

CONTENT TIP:

MODIFY MEDIA TOP TIPS

Post a branded or watermarked image: Posting a funny or inspirational image with your logo or website URL on it, could gain you more traction from that images reach. If that image is shared elsewhere, then your brand will follow.

YouTube tasks & notes..

Have you connected with other YouTubers and considered collaboration work?

(One of the fastest ways to grow on YouTube is collaboration work)

Does your meta data, aka back end information match your title and
description to give you the best chance of being searched for on YouTube?

(All your descriptions, titles, tags and file names help towards being discovered on YouTube, make sure to optimise your wording)

Have you considered a weekly video, or regular video content to help be consistent on YouTube?

(Quality content in king, although consistent content is key.
Consistency is key to YouTube growth, as well as networking with other YouTubers. Make sure you are releasing constant content for your subscribers)

Are you contributing to your industry, through regular interactions on other peoples content?

(A key to growth on social media is being actively involved in not only your own content, but contributing and redistributing other peoples content. This includes commenting and getting involved in other peoples discussions)

NOTES:

Instagram

The visual leader in social media, obviously owned by the real leader in social media 'Facebook'. Instagram has really blossomed since being taken over by the social media giant Facebook back in 2012.

There could be a argument that Pinterest is very similar to Instagram, as it is another visual based social media platform, meaning images and videos. Both have endless streams of limitless information that are displayed in a scrolling interface.

The big difference is Instagram is much like many social media applications, as you scroll up and show the limitless amount of status, posts, pictures, videos from the brands, businesses and people you follow.

Pinterest however have added a visual twist to their layout, as they have decided to give more variety with their endless stream of information. Pinterest actually show multiple posts, similar to a endless digital pin board. As you scroll up you will see more and more multiple posts, of which may lead to a higher interest and can get people scrolling longer out of curiosity.

One main reason Instagram beats Pinterest is because it was here first. People have dedicated time and effort to build their Instagram accounts, so any new social media platform to come along has to be amazing to break that time invested into that social media platform.

This is true with any social media account created, its the time, effort, attachment, followers and relationships built that many users find hard to break away from.

Take a look at Facebook for instance, so many people say "Im deleting this app" in hopes that they can stay away, but social media addiction brings them right back.

As you also know Instagram is owned by Facebook, so many of the business related services available are also linked to the Facebook platform.

When you share a image or video on Instagram, you have the easy one button option to instantly share that content straight to your Facebook page. Sharing on Instagram and Facebook at the same time, with the same content is a win in its own right, but there is more from the social media leaders.

Both Instagram and Facebook have 'Stories' of which is very similar to snapchats feature where you can create stories for people to watch and interact with, but these stories will vanish within 24 hours time.

Instagram also has the added 'Live' feature that you can find within your 'Stories' section. Live video started out on Facebook and has been a huge success on all the social media platforms that have followed suit.

Social media platforms such as Twitter and YouTube also have this added live feature, but in true fashion Facebook is the leader once again with the amount of live videos posted daily.

Instagram is a winning social media platform for the simple business boosting post ability, right down to the easy share ability of your Instagram posts to external platforms.

Instagram also have a great feature of which lets you become a amateur photographer, well sort of when it first started.
The filters on Instagram was big news, but now it seems every social media platform has adapted to give filters to your images.

ENGAGMENT TIP:

MODIFY MEDIA TOP TIPS

A controversial blog post, or social media post: There's nothing better for increasing engagement than a little controversy. Keep it clean, but make sure to get a tasteful debate going.

It goes down in the DM's!

As we all know by now networking on social media was the true reason 'social' media was created. Social media aka social networks.. Unfortunately we have lost touch with even the simple task of networking online, but trust me when I say, you need to get personal.

What do I mean by personal? Simple.
Spark a conversation, even try that strange thing called being social..
Yes talk to people on Instagram, drop some comments and even drop a DM (Direct Message). If you feel you want to connect with someone on Instagram, don't be afraid to drop them a direct message.
It shows that you have taken the time out to reach further then the casual comment or post like.

People don't connect with brands or businesses, they connect with other people.
People sell to people, its not the product or service that sells its self. If you feel you could collaborate with another business then contact them and put forward your suggestions.
If you want to thank a customer for their comments, their interactions, or their loyalty, then drop them a thank you DM.

If there are people you want to connect with and build relationships with, then the best way to do this is get personal with those you want to be connected with. Take your networking to the next level and reach out to others on Instagram.

Leaving comments and interacting with your followers comments are great, but don't forget if you want that relationship or that winning idea to go further then a few comments you need to reach out. Instagram DM may be your new email... We suggest you still email, but remember if they are active on social media then reach out on social media.

ENGAGMENT TIP:

MODIFY MEDIA TOP TIPS

Ask for input on your products, or services: Your followers will like giving their thoughts on how to improve your products, or services. This can also be taken as market research or feedback.

A quality Instagram post

As you are fully aware from the Facebook quality post example, there are some essentials when posting on social media.
Location is great as it lets other users know where you and your business are, or where you have been.
Tagging of other businesses, people and brands is also a great way to maximise your reach on social media.

Instagram is very similar to Facebook, but a quality post on both social media platforms have some essentials and differences.
Facebook users rarely use hashtags, where as Instagram users love them.
Hashtags are so popular on Instagram that you will receive 50% higher response rate for hash tagged content.

Hash tag tip: Save your hashtags in your notes on your phone, this way you don't have to keep remembering and writing them out for each post. Simply find roughly 20+ hashtags that relate to your business and once you have them write them out in your notes for use with your future posts. Also remember its a good idea to start your own hashtag, for example we have #MODIFYMEDIA Starting your own hashtag will help your customers find your content at a later date.

Example of quality Instagram post:

modify_media
Eastbourne, East Sussex

Tagging your location is vital, especially if you are to do business within that area. You will want local customers to be aware of your business.

Tagging businesses, people and brands is always a good way to boost engagement on Instagram. This also shows a mutual respect and relationship to those involved within the post.

View Insights

Promote

Liked by **mrfatztv, wepushducks** and 22 others

modify_media Don't forget we are the No.1 choice for friendly helpful advice! 😄
Photographer & owner: @mrfatztv
We also provide:
Social media management
Photography
Videography
Web design
Team training
Social media marketing

.

#socialmedia #socialmediamarketing #business #twitter #facebook #youtube #instagram #networking #sussex #modifymedia #eastbourne #eastsussex #brighton #hastings #marketing #photography #videography #productions

Hashtags are essential on Instagram, they are one of the best ways to stand out. You are allowed to post up to 30 hashtags.

NETWORKING TIP:

——— MODIFY MEDIA TOP TIPS ———

Share third party content related to your industry as a way to build your own brand identity.

99

Instagram top tips

- Image quality - Instagram is a image based social media platform. If you are posting images of your business, especially of products it would pay to learn some basic photography techniques on lighting, angles and affects.
  You can use your mobile phone for your images, but take the time to make a effort with your posts. Your images represent your business.

- Hashtags - Hash tagging is essential on Instagram more then any other social media platform. Hashtags started out on Twitter, but become a must do on Instagram. You are allowed to hashtag up to 30 times per post on Instagram and we suggest you hashtag over 20 at least. Stay clear of generic 'spam' hashtags such as #followforfollow #likeforlike as these will weaken your brand and could get you a shadow ban. A shadow ban is a way of Instagram limiting your visibility from other users, to which will lower your engagement.

- The description - A good write up or description underneath each image will show how much care and detail you put into your posts.
  Your follows and potential followers will react more positively to a well written description of the image. Bullet points, entertainment and information are all great for Instagram posts. Asking a question in the caption is a great way to increase engagement.

- Tagging - Tagging your location is essential if you are to allow your potential customers/ followers to find your business. Tagging and hash tagging the location and surrounding locations, is a great way to get local exposure. Always tag people who feature in your posts, if someone has interacted with your business it would also be good practice to tag them in relevant posts to thank them or do a shout out.

- Get involved - Building a following is fairly easy on social media, but getting the right followers who interact and increase engagement on your posts is a lot harder.
You need to start building relationships, whilst your building a following. If you have some dedicated followers who engage, then make sure you are engaging back with them.
Build relationships with like minded people. If you want to collaborate with people, or business then shoot over a DM (direct message). Real engagement and loyal followers, will always be better then a larger following who never interact with content.

- Keep up the momentum - One of the worst ways to dwindle out your Instagram account, is to stop your activity. Whilst it is great having new content for Instagram profile and you post everyday for a whole month, remember if you start slowing down your account will suffer.
Lack of content losses followers, its a harsh truth on many social media platforms. Who wants to follow a dead account?..

Instagram tasks & notes..

Have you saved the relevant hash tags to relate to your industry, as well as your own hash tags?

(Instagram posts perform best when you maximise your hash tag usage, so make sure you save those hash tags on your phone for use on each post.)

Instagram is one of the easiest platforms to network on, how much time each day are you using to network within your industry?

(Simply searching for relevant hash tags and commenting/engaging with those in your industry can build relationship and brand strength)

Are you getting personal with those in your industry?

(It goes down in the direct messages. Being personal and connecting through direct message can really help strengthen your online engagement and relationships, whilst also opening doors for potential collaboration work)

Quality posting is key to growth on Instagram, how much effort are you putting into each post?

(Each post should have a location, hash tags and tagging the people, brands or businesses involved in each post)

NOTES:

Snapchat

Snapchat has grown rapidly since its launch in 2011, with many celebrities and businesses leveraging the use of this quick snap mobile app. Initially you could assume that a quick video or images that disappear wouldn't be much good for a business, but you would be wrong.

So many more people want to be closer and more connected to their favourite celebrity or even brand now days, that they take to social media to do so. Snap chat has allowed followers to feel closer to celebrities, businesses and brands, by giving them a behind the scenes feel. A personal snapchat touch as it would seem.

Snapchat has proven its worth in the social media world with a outstanding reach of over 150 million users everyday. Whilst we are talking numbers lets take in the fact that the app has over a astonishing 400 million snaps sent every single day.
You may also like to know that on average users open the app roughly 18 times within a day.
Another exciting fact is, snapchat reaches roughly 40% of 18 - 34 year olds in the US alone..
Now think about your target market and how you could leverage the power of this social media app?..

You may have noticed that many other social media apps, such as Facebook and Instagram have now used such features as stories, which utilise the quick videos or images. But snapchat users have not been put off by this and rightly so, snapchat users love the fact that they have another means of communication.

Also remember the emotional attachment with social media platforms, once someone has dedicated time becoming familiar with a platform and invested their time and effort building a following it is very hard for individuals to let go of that commitment, the content, or the following. The invested time into building a following on social media platforms is one reason, so many 'new' social media apps try and fail to attract a large user base.

Why you should choose the quick snap app..

Snapchat as mentioned has well over 150 million active daily users, sending well over 400 million daily snaps. If your not apart of that growing action, then you may want to start getting involved real soon.
No one wants to be left in the past and it is clear from the sheer numbers side of this social media network, that snapchat is a growing beyond all once conceived beliefs.

The emotional and personal attachments people hold to businesses, brands and celebrities is what drives repeat business and a larger following.
You need to win your customer over and what better way at doing this, then becoming closer to your customers.
There are many ways to connect with these businesses and brands but none like the snapchat app.
You do have features on other social media platforms, of which are very similar to the snapchat social media app but they simply are not the snappy app.
Once people become accustom to using a social media app, it is very hard to get them to stop using it.

Lets say for example you are running a competition exclusively on snapchat, of which only those who are really connected will be able to take part in.
Whilst this competition is running, you can then

get your snapchat followers to share the competition on their social media accounts.
A simple "screen shot the next snap and tag us on Facebook, we will announce the winner in one week" type competition will get you on their social media account and also get others intrigued into what is hidden on your snapchat business account. You will attract new snappers, as well as growing your brand.

Another great competition to run is, "Send us your wackiest snap and the winner will be given _ _ _ _ _ _". This type of competition gets your snapchat followers interacting with your brand as well as giving you content to post on other social media platforms, then choosing a winner.

There are loads of other competitions or exclusives you can run through snapchat, of which only dedicated followers will see. This allows your snapchat followers fell a sense of authority, or exclusivity that may help you stand out from the crowed.

ENGAGMENT TIP:

MODIFY MEDIA TOP TIPS

Encourage conversation by asking people questions. The reason for this is when people answer your questions, that content reaches further on social media.

Snapchat tasks & notes..

Are you giving exclusive behind the scenes footage to your followers through snapchat?

(Snapchat is used to give a personal behind the scenes touch to influencers, celebrities, businesses and brands)

Have you tried to do a exclusive competition to attract more people to interact and follow your business, or brand on snapchat?

(Snapchats exclusive and connective touch helps people feel closer to the businesses and brands they follow, of which many businesses utilise, to run competitions attracting more snapchat followers)

Notes..

Content marketing

Content marketing is a type of marketing that involves creating high-quality content, of which is valuable, engaging and informative.
The high-quality content should attract a large audience, whilst also promoting a brand, product, or service.

If done right content marketing is the process of stimulate the interest of individuals, to a standard of which they would distribute your content for you in many cases.
The distribution of your content would be through increased engagement, liking, following and practically sharing your content as it is seen to be of interest, value, or entertaining.

Content marketing increases brand preference, of which helps establish your brand as a authority within your industry. Increased authority within your industry will help strengthen your brand/ business and attract that larger audience you desire.

Look at content marketing as your number one choice to advertise for FREE, yes thats right it is a perfect way to spread your brand or business for free if done right.

Many businesses create lets say a video advert and post in to social media, then pay to boost it locally to increase engagement in hopes of making some sales or getting some attention for their business.

Now imagine that video was so entertaining that people wanted to share and tag their friends so they also see this entertaining video.

Perhaps the video was so educational that people who have seen it are astounded with what they have learnt, so they decide they want to tag and share it with their friends.

This is content marketing done right, it is your quality content getting the traction it deserves from the time and effort you put into crating this piece of content.

SNAPCHAT TIP:

MODIFY MEDIA TOP TIPS

Be a human on snapchat. This is not the platform on which to talk about 'Business, marketing techniques and non stop product drives'. Create some entertaining or engaging content for your snapchat followers to enjoy.

Example of content marketing:

Hair Salon One

ATTRACTING
IRREGULAR SALES

Hair salon one is a standard hairdressing salon, of which is based in a small town. They use their online social media platforms to pay for advertising on various posts, such as: '10% off this weekend'. They have their regular customers and attract a irregular few customers through some online advertising.

Hair salon one has a big problem here, as they are posting nothing but sales, offers and irregular pictures or statuses across their social media platforms. Not only does the irregular posting reduce your reach on social media, but also may bore your current followers who do not feel the need or desire to interact with your content.

Many businesses fall into this category of irregular boring posts and over selling on social media.

Hair Salon Two

• INCREASED ENGAGEMENT
• INCREASED REACHABILITY
• INCREASED SALES

Hair salon two is also a standard hairdressing salon based in a small town, identical situation as hair salon one.
Hair salon two also post some sales and offers, just like hair salon one.

The difference with hair salon two is the other content they are distributing to their audience. Hair salon two creates a video once a week, such as tutorials, product reviews, services updates and other useful information for their audience.

Hair salon two also regularly post, or shares other larger hair companies posts.
They are sure that the external content they share is kept relatable to the services they offer.
This content marketing strategy on hair salon two's social media platforms would produce a increase in engagement, distribution and likability from around the town and further.

Hair salon two would be sharing useful insightful tips, ideas and tutorials, of which would make hair salon two a more authoritative figure within the hairdressing industry.

As you can imagine this way of marketing your business is fantastic for gaining more engagement on social media. You will attract more clientele, who would see you as leading authority within your marketplace.

ENGAGMENT TIP:

Be Picky About What You Share on social media, keep your followers in mind when you are creating or sharing content.

· Is it relevant to your audience
· Is it helpful
· Is it entertaining
· Is it informative

JAB, JAB, RIGHT HOOK

If you have ever heard of Gary Vaynerchuk, you will know he is a social media influencer and very successful entrepreneur.

Gary has released some amazing books and video content, but one theory that has resonated with us is the '**Jab, Jab, Right Hook**'.

The concept behind Jab, Jab, Right Hook is giving great quality content again and again and again, then asking or selling something.

This asking for something in return is your right hook, but you only do this once you have given a lot of value.

Jab, jab, jab, right hook = Give, give, give, then ask.

Giving more value out on social media will attract a lot more engagement on your platforms and posts.

The more you give, the higher the chance will be that when you do finally ask for something from your following you will receive it.

News jacking

News jacking is the art and science of injecting your brand or business into a breaking headline story, so that you can generate media and social media attention towards your business.
The simple idea of jumping on the bandwagon taking someone else's story and attaching yourself to it, this is done to increase exposure whilst the story is still a hot topic.

For a good example, when it was a hot topic that the new iPhones bent easily in your back pocket, KitKat actually brought out a advert of which stated:

"We don't bend, we break"

This short but cheeky dig was towards iPhones hot news story at the time. KitKat went a step further and displayed a image of a KitKat bending at a 45 degree angle. As you can see from this example many top brands use news jacking for extra exposure of their own brand.

If you are to news hijack, then we suggest you do it tastefully as to not attract negative attention. The last thing you would want to do is create a piece of content, or a offer that would make fun or attach your business to a emotional negative story in the news.

The day after the tragedy of the Boston bombings a food company (we will not name) tweeted:

"Boston, our hearts are with you. Here's a bowl of breakfast energy we could all use today"

They also added a link to this tweet... This is a bad example of news jacking. Although they may have had good intentions, it. is never a good idea to try and news jack a tragedy, or negative emotional news.

As you can imagine some times when you are trying to news hack, you have to get very creative with what you do and say to relate back to the original story. If done right your news hacking campaign or advert has the possibility of attract a very large audience.

The famous and very adventurous entrepreneur Richard Branson has been international headline news on various occasions, although he was news jacking he was jacking the news headlines and creating he's own top story. You may be thinking if he's not news jacking then what use is it in the content marketing section of this book!?

Simple he was jacking the news headlines to gain international exposure for he's stunt, or adventurous, flamboyant behaviour.
But the reason behind he's headlines are more creative then the actual adventures. Richard Branson the billionaire and owner of Virgin, grabs a lot of news headlines because its cheaper then advertising internationally.

Think about this for a second. You want to advertise your billion dollar company around the world so people switch to your air line, but you have just found out that advertising at that level will cost over 40 million world wide. Now a huge

world record stunt, or adventure would only cost 10 million to grab headlines world wide...
Surly the 10 million to grab front page headlines world wide would seem the cheaper and more exciting route to take. Thats a form of news jacking, with your own story and own twist to grab the desired attention.

ENGAGMENT TIP:

MODIFY MEDIA TOP TIPS

Fill in the blank posts, are similar to question posts..
(e.g. "If I had $1 million I would _____")
This is a great way to increase engagement, buy giving the power to the follower to complete your post in their own words.

Addicted

Social media addiction has swept a generation, with nearly every youngster glued to a mobile device of some sort. We live in a age where if you have a mobile phone, the chances are you have a slight addiction to some sort of ego feeding social media platform.

This social media craze is sweeping the globe with billions online, yet we have grown more unconnected as a race.
With the rise of social media usage, there has been a drop in human contact on a face to face level. Increasing amounts of people choose to talk online, rather then in person as they have a boost in confidence.

Another factor to social media is our shopping habits, its clear to see the rise in online consumption with the likes of Amazon, Netflix and Ebay. Our shopping habits are highly influenced through social media, have you ever been scrolling on social media to see a advert of something you may have searched for recently!?

This strange coincidence is no coincidence, it is all down to retarget marketing and using user habits and interests. Companies are targeting millions through social media, because they know you are addicted and they will get straight onto your newsfeed. They use your interests and recent searches to display the products or services that

may peak your interest to purchase.
Don't worry, you can also use this addiction to
your advantage. You can target your desired
consumer the exact same way large companies
are targeting you!

Here are some surprising statistics, that will make
you think twice about your own addiction to social
media:

- Roughly 5 million images are uploaded to
  Instagram, daily.

- 45% of social media users check their timeline
  whilst eating.

- Over 55% of younger social media users
  check their accounts on mobiles devices.

- 37% of students admitted that their social
  media updates, held more interest then their
  classroom studies.

- Over 3 hours everyday is spent on social
  media for users aged 15-19.

- Over 66% of users are checking their social
  media apps from bed, with studies suggesting
  this is affecting their sleeping habits.

- 60 - 80% of peoples time on the internet at
  work has nothing to do with work.

- Over 20% of social media users can't go for a
  few hours without checking their social media
  apps.

- Over 60% of Facebook users have to check
  their Facebook account at least once a day.

- 28% of iPhone users who own a twitter account, check their twitter feed before they get out of bed.

- 4 out of 5 students feel negative emotions and side affects if they are disconnected from technology for more then a day.

- Majority of student with social media accounts admit that they would not go without social media for more then 24hours, if they had a choice.

ENGAGMENT TIP:

MODIFY MEDIA TOP TIPS

Cover these principles in your next post to help it go viral:
Positive, secret, funny, stunning, exceptional, outrageous, taboo

Do you have a social media addiction problem?

If so, are you, your target market?
Answering these questions and analysing your own use of social media, you could be able to gauge where and when your target audience will see your posts online.

Often in a business, the business owner is passionate about the product or service they are offering to potential customers.
That is why in many cases, your own social media usage can be taken into account when finding your target market. Looking at your own addiction of what platforms you are using, may help determine where your target market will be.

Please bare in mind many people are different, so here is a rough idea of your potential target market and their online activities:

- Linked in - 79% of users are over 35years old.

- Snapchat - 71% of users are under 34 years old.

- Instagram - 90% of users are under 35 years old.

- YouTube - 82% of users are teenagers.

- Pintrest - 80% are female users.

- Facebook - 88% of users are between 18-29 years old.

- Linked in - Considered on of the most professional social media sites.

- Snapchat - Has the youngest demographic.

- Twitter - Noticed as one of the best sources for news reports and upcoming news.

- Facebook - One of the easiest sites to share links, with over 1 million links shared every 20 minutes.

- Facebook - Best times to post is between 1pm-4pm.

- Wednesday afternoon is considered the most active time on social media.

TIMING TIP:

 MODIFY MEDIA TOP TIPS

Your social media marketing content dies after a while, so it is always good practice to know the best time to post. If you want to maximise exposure, be sure to research your target market and catch them at the best times.

Email is not dead!

Social media is everywhere, everyone has it, or know's someone who is addicted to it. Social media is one of the greatest advancements to ever hit the internet!

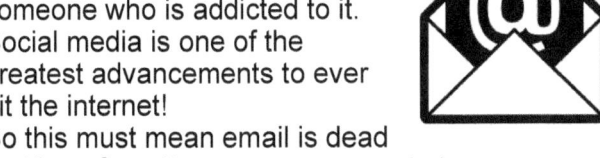

So this must mean email is dead and long forgotten, as no one wants to use a primitive tool of communication anymore!?...

Wrong!
Email is still thriving and rightly so, email is still seen as one of the best and most used ways of communication amongst professionals.
Emailing not only allows a greater chance of connectivity and privacy, but it is still seen as the number one communication tool within business to date.
Stay professional and stick to emailing your clients, customers and other professionals.

Email is here to stay, so get used to it.
Did you know that, there is over 74 trillion emails sent every year?
That number is still growing each year..
Over 90% adults in the US actively use email, of which is not just a adult 'thing'.
74% of teenagers are also actively using email.

Another way to look at it is, when you sign up to a new mobile contract, or a new gym membership, what contact details do they prefer having?
Perhaps you are applying for a new job, or

booking a holiday, what contact details do they nearly demand every time?
Its certainly not your twitter link, or Instagram name.

EMAIL MARKETING TIP:

Offer coupon code in exchange for a visitor's email address.
The coupons can be discounts for products, or services you sell on your site.
You don't need to discount a lot, just enough to encourage people to sign up or opt-in to your email list.

Email marketing affects us all

Lets keep it simple for those who are unaware of what email marketing is. Email marketing is a form of direct marketing that utilises the power of electronic mail to communicate with prospective clients and customers.

Business owners use email marketing as a tool to encourage repeat of in cases new customers to purchase their product or service. Whilst email marketing is simple it is highly effective when it comes to building a relationships through email contact.

Emailing allows businesses to reach out to potential customers with personalised, relevant and dynamic messages.
This is also great news if someone has signed up to a 'Opt-in' section, yet abandoned their purchase before paying for your product or service. You can then retarget this customer with a quick friendly email reminding them of their interest.

Email marketing reaches its intended recipient, of which the statistics suggest a estimated 98% of emails are delivered. Now look at your social media reach and deliverability. With social media you have to time out and plan each post to maximise your reach of which is still not guaranteed.

If someone has not been interacting with your social media platform, then it is highly unlikely that you will be able to get onto their newsfeed with

your content.
But if someone ignores your social media platform, you can guarantee you can still get their attention through a email, of which may spark their interest back to your social media platforms.

Reconnecting with your clients and customers is big business in email marketing, thats why so many social media entrepreneurs have multiple email sign up forms.
Opt-in forms as they are also known.

You are guaranteed to reach a customer with a good social media strategy and email marketing strategy combined.

Email marketing affects us all from many spam emails filling up your junk box, to emails relating to phone insurance for the new mobile phone contract you have just signed.
Companies usually use email marketing to redirect sales back to previous customers, this is one reason that many businesses ask for your email addresses. Statistics suggest that customers who have used a product or service before are more likely to repurchase.

You can use the power of email marketing in your business, with platforms and software such as MailChimp, Infusionsoft and many other services available.
Many of these services are free when you first start to use them, so why not get involved in email marketing today.
All it takes is a little time, effort, knowledge and signing up with your very own email address..

Email marketing / Content marketing (The Drip)

As mention email is still thriving today, especially email marketing. So after reading this short chapter on Email marketing we hope you utilise this information and get a great strategy in place to maximise your reach online.

Here is a Email marketing technique to use to keep your followers engaged and up to date with your brand. This technique (The Drip) also comes under the category of being a content marketing technique, which is fantastic news for you the business owner.

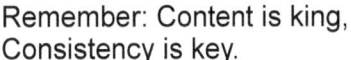

Remember: Content is king, Consistency is key.

Your 'Drip' technique is a way off keeping your clients, customers and followers engaged through email marketing.
Keeping up momentum is a great way to keep your social media platforms active as well as keeping people up to date with the business they have opted in to hear about.

Sending out a weekly email to each and every person who has opted in for your updates can be extremely time consuming, of which as a business owner you simply do not have the time and resources to do individually.
So you simply do it through automation.

A automatic sequence of pre written emails sent out weekly, will allow you to keep your followers up to date and engaged.

Be sure your weekly drip is exciting, entertaining, or informative as this will have a positive effect on those on the receiving end of this email marketing technique.

Try not to be so sales orientated, this way you will build up relationships and brand strength that you can use for sales down the line.
Refer back to content marketing section of this book and think about the jab, jab, jab, hook method of marketing.

You can set up pre automated emails through Mailchimp or Infusionsoft, amongst other Email marketing systems.
This automation drip keeps everyone happy and saves time once it has been set up.

A great idea is to have a system where you send a weekly email in relation to the way they opted in for your email marketing.
For example, lets say that someone has opted in to receive updates through one of your email funnels or Opt-ins.
They signed up for a free ebook on Facebook use, yet you've automatically signed them up for 4 weeks of free automated emails related to advertising information on Facebook.

This type of related automation emailing will be of interest to your follower who signed up for the Facebook ebook.
Now you have a potential customer fully engaged for one month, who will also be receiving free

information and happy with the initial ebook.
That is a lot of free value you have given out with
one ebook offer.

After all this you have another happy customer
who may be more willing to purchase a product or
service down the line, through one of your emails.

Here is a idea of why email is still massive today:

- Privacy is big business in business. Email
  communication adds a aspect of privacy and
  exclusivity to your communication.

- The concept of sending multiple files of which
  lose no quality when sent. Email and cloud
  drives are still one of the highest forms of
  documentation sending.

- The professional feel and quality of
  communication appears to be more desired
  via email.

- Many businesses and professionals refer back
  to a email for notes, or proof of an order/
  purchase.

- Email marketing is huge business, if you have
  ever been sent a offer or 'exclusive' webinar.
  Then you have been on the receiving end of
  someones email marketing plan.

- Research shows that old-fashioned email is
  still far more affective then social media.

Mobile is winning

If your website is not mobile friendly, then your website is already failing for your business. This is the bare minimum every company or business should be doing, making sure that everything they produce or display can be accessed by a mobile device.

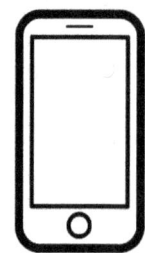

Did you know that by 2019 it is expected that mobile users will exceed the five billion mark. You may also like to know that as a populace we are already over the 60% user mark, thats well over half the worlds population already on mobile devices.
If you think how far technology has come and where it is heading, then you would be deemed crazy to think these statistic do not apply to you and your business.

Just like the addicted part of this book, not only is social media a massive addiction problem but mobile usage alone is a huge addictive attribute in todays society.

Worryingly over 60% of mobile phone users check their mobile phone for calls and texts, without their phone making a sound.
This indicates a constant urge to use or misuse your mobile device, of which a business owner can really use to their advantage.

Have you ever heard of 'Nomophobia'?
This is the technical term for the irrational fear of being without use of your mobile device. Low battery, no signal, broken phone, these are part of the phobia.
A phobia is by definition an irrational fear.
Although its not all doom and gloom, this addiction is massive for you a business owner.

EMAIL MARKETING TIP:

MODIFY MEDIA TOP TIPS

Give your subscribers something for free to gain more trust and show it is worth staying signed up for your newsletter.
Often people hard sell, whi

Here is where you can be winning on mobile

Why would someone go shopping for a new pair of socks, when two clicks on a mobile phone and it will be delivered in a couple of days..
Buying the socks or any item online usually costs less then heading to the local town to do a days worth of shopping, wasting valuable time, money and effort.

A quick search on the mobile device, whilst relaxing in a hot bath can be all the shopping experience needed, this would also be clearing that task of buying socks from the persons to do list.
Convenience is key here, if it is a simple process people generally like it more.

If you as a business owner can utilise this information and ease the effort of buying, then you will be winning. You need to imagine with simplicity, that you are affectively making your customers lives easier.
Wether they need a product, service, or even a visit from a specialist the easier the task through a mobile device the higher the chance of regular custom.

Many people buy the same product over and over, which is all fantastic news if you can get the initial sale in the first place.
You need to remember as a business owner once you have a sale, then you can retarget market to that customer.

Using email marketing, text alerts, or even a complementary phone call.
A customer who has bought a product or service with ease online is more likely to repurchase.

If you have a product or service that can be sold online, then you have a duty to make the process as easy as possible.
Automation is key, baring in mind simplicity and connectivity, especially for mobile users.
It would be a huge benefit to the growth of your business, if you could make it convenient to quickly purchase your product or service.

You could argue some like the idea of actually going shopping, getting close to the products they are buying. This is true, but in broader sense this is also not applicable to simple items such as socks, body wash, aftershave, laptops, phones, new stationary, etc.

Yes people like trying on clothes and seeing sizes, but much of what we purchase can be bought online faster, cheaper and easier.
Online shopping is only rising, with many big high street retail brands either adapting to the changing shopping habits, or going bust due to lack of business.

K I S S = Keep It Simple, Stupid

Kiss was initially used by the US navy in the 1960's as a acronym of keep it simple stupid.
A system or marketing in many cases usually works best when the process or system is kept simple. The less complex the design the higher the chances of success.

Network = Net Worth

Have you ever heard that saying your network equals your net worth. You know the saying in many films, especially law or gangster films "Its not what you know, its who you know" Well business is similar to the movies, just with less gangsters.

Your network can greatly attribute to your success on and offline. Many business owners regular attend networking events, or join networking clubs to 'network' with likeminded individuals.

Your network can greatly increase your chances of success, although your network should be relative to your niche or industry you are actively involved in. Revert back to the Facebook section of this book, where we talked about digital footprints and networking.

Online can be seen as a big scary world, especially if your not internet savvy. Social media, website optimisation, automation and much much more can be a daunting task for any business owner looking to grow online.

Your lack of knowledge on a certain aspect could be someones strength, so think of it this way the more people you network with, the greater the chances of success.

If you create relationships with a vast amount of people in your industry you will be seen as a industry leader, due to your network and the content you are creating and sharing of others.

As you network with others you will automatically be building brand strength through these interactions and opening the doors to new ideas. Possibly new collaborative projects with those you have networked with.
Another good quote to remember is:
"Team work, makes the dream work"

As you begin to network or connect more with others, you subconsciously learn new ways to conduct yourself online.
How someone else is selling a product may be a slightly different marketing plan to your own, but producing double the sales.

One of the greatest aspects of doing what we do, is the simple and effective task of networking. You cant be afraid to reach out to those in your niche. Stop seeing those in your industry as competition and start networking today.
The first rule of friendship, or high influence is; 'Make others feel good about themselves'.

EMAIL MARKETING TIP:

MODIFY MEDIA TOP TIPS

Don't be afraid to send a thank you, or appreciation email to your followers. A simple positive message, quote, or image to brighten their day may keep your brand in a positive category for them.

Networking in your community

You have a niche or a industry, as a business owner you have competition and customers interested in your brand, product, or service.
These are the people you will want to connect with, you will want to become apart of their community, this is on each and every platform.

It is simple business if you sell fishing rods, then your community is the people who are passionate about fishing, your niche is fishing, your industry is fishing.

In theory your community or potential customers are going to be in fishing groups on Facebook, they will be hash tagging fishing content on Instagram, they will be tweeting about fishing on Twitter.
This is where you step in and get active in the community, this is you networking!

Your potential customers will be loading up images and videos everywhere, all relating back to your industry or niche of which in this case is fishing.
Start commenting on their posts, start getting involved within their conversations online.

If you want to maximise your reach and improve your engagement, then you need to start engaging yourself on social media.

All to often we are posting or selling on social media, without being social and using a social networking app for what it was made for.
Start networking daily and you will see the positive effects of effective networking.

You need to spend some time everyday finding other peoples content revolving around your niche or industry, then engaging with that content to build relationships.
If you do this everyday, you will soon start getting followers, likes and increased engagement through your initial engaging. Don't be afraid to get stuck in on other peoples content, its been posted online for a reason.

Bring value to your community, so when someone finds your comment or post they value your brand for the content you have create.

For example if someones looking for a bait idea in fishing, then give them some options you know about, even some links or ideas of what others are using.
This sort of interacting is helpful and valuable at the same time, of which helps support you as becoming a authority within that community.

This sort of activity and participation works in every niche or industry, trust us go try out and become apart of your community. It will increase your growth drastically.

Tips for networking

- Complements will go further then criticism. If you see a business in your industry or niche that you may like to connect with, make sure you make a great first impression with a positive statement or complement. There is a saying of which states first impressions are key to building relationships.
Before you start talking to your person of interest, make sure to let them know you are no threat by sharing their content, leaving positive comments and mentioning their business. This will all help towards building a positive rapport when you decide to make direct contact.

- Become connected and fearless. Many business owners constantly see other business owners as threats or competition, especially those in the same industry.
If you are constantly scared and fearful of other business owners, then you lack the power to utilise their business to boost yours..
Networking is about supporting each other, whilst learning new skills along the way.

- If you are a hair salon and know of a beauty salon, we suggest you drop your ego and massively connect! Share each others content online, share each others leaflets or promotions in store. You could even go as far as 10% discount for each others customers, which is highly attractive offer seeing as you are likely to share customers.
We've left a good list below, highlighting some

businesses that could potentially support each other:

Gym owners + Health shops
Car mechanics + Car salesmen
Hair salons + Beauty salons
Media production companies + Photographers
Graphic designers + Print companies

CONTENT MARKETING TIP:

MODIFY MEDIA TOP TIPS

Don't be afraid to send a thank you, or appreciation email to your followers. A simple positive message, quote, or image to brighten their day may keep your brand in a positive category for them.

References

- **Call to action** - Within marketing a call to action is a direct instruction to the audience, to which provokes a fast response. Usually relating to: "Call now", "Message us today", or "Book a appointment, to secure your place".

- **Social networking** - The simplistic form of social network is the main aim of using social media.

- **Content marketing** - This is a form of marketing, by creating valuable content such as video, blogs, images, or social media posts. This created content helps build your brand, whilst attracting engagement and stimulating interest for your product or service.

- **Viral** - Referring to a piece of content, such as video, blog, images, or posts. Content going viral is a piece of content gaining a large amount of interactions, from user to user and circulating the internet rapidly.

- **Investment** - The action or process of investing money for profit. Also be aware of time investment in similar circumstances, which would relate to time being spent for the purpose of profit or future gain.

- **Spam** - Spamming is easy on social media, both real people and bots regularly use social media platforms to spam. Spamming is the process of sharing the same content indiscriminately, with a large number of internet users.

- **Meta Data** - Meta data is a set of data that describes and gives information about other data.
  Meta data is a kind of behind the scenes or back end data that describes or gives extra information on your original content. Using Meta Data correctly can help boost your SEO

- **SEO** - Search engine optimisation is essentially the process of maximising the number of visitors to a particular website.
  This is done by ensuring that the site appears high on the list of results returned by a search engine.

- **Social media marketing** - Social media marketing is the use of social media platforms to promote a business, brand, product or service.
  You can use your social media platforms data analytics to track the effectiveness of each social media marketing technique you use, in your adverts and campaigns.

- **Social media or website analytics** - These analytics are the systematic usage of various data received on either a social media platform or website. You can use this data or analytics to improve your engagement and marketing/ advertising campaigns.
  Some times referred to as data analysis.

Connect with us at Modify Media

We hope this book and some of our FREE video content has helped improve your business online. Modify Media and its team are dedicated to supporting businesses both on and offline, so please connect with us and let us support you further.

You will find Modify Media through the hashtag #MODIFYMEDIA or you can search Modify Media on any search engine, alternatively you can find us at:

www.facebook.com/modifymedia

www.twitter.com/modifymedia

www.instagram.com/modify_media

If you would like to connect with the owner of modify media and serial entrepreneur you can at @MRFATZTV or #MRFATZTV
Alternatively you can find him at:

www.facebook.com/mrfatztv

www.twitter.com/mrfatztv

www.instagram.com/mrfatztv

Thank you for your time, we hope this book can help you succeed online.